GRIEVING THE LOSS OF A LOVE

HOW TO EMBRACE GRIEF TO FIND HOPE AND HEALING AFTER A DIVORCE, BREAKUP, OR DEATH

ELEORA HAN, PHD

KOMOREBI PRESS

Komorebi Press, LLC
1069 West Broad Street, Suite 804
Falls Church, VA 22046

Copyright © 2017 by Eleora Han, PhD

ISBN (Paperback): 978-1-948190-00-8
ISBN (eBook): 978-1-948190-01-5
Author Photo: Authentic Portrait
Cover Design: Zeeshan Shams

Each of the case studies presented in this book are constructed as a character study based on a combination of real people (rather than any one person specifically), with all names, identifying information, and characteristics significantly changed to protect privacy.

This book is not intended as a substitute for the medical recommendations of physicians, mental health professionals, or other healthcare providers. Rather, it is intended to offer accurate information to help the reader cooperate with physicians, mental health professionals, and health providers in a mutual pursuit of health and well-being. If medical advice or other expert counseling and help are needed, the services of an appropriate health professional should be sought.

To all the people in my life
who, over the years,
taught me
about life and love.
Thank you.

I don't think of all the misery,

but of all the beauty that remains.

— ANNE FRANK

INTRODUCTION

I am grateful you have found this book so that we can walk together on this part of your life's journey. Few events in life are more difficult than losing a loved one, whether through death, a painful breakup, or divorce. Losing someone we love disrupts the very foundation and fabric of our lives. It shatters our understanding of the world and throws us into deep grief and devastation.

I wrote this book after the loss of my husband from divorce. Our separation was sudden and unexpected. With the loss of him came many other significant losses: his smile, kindness, and sense of humor; the sound of his voice as he greeted me upon arriving home. We had been together for nearly half my life when we said our good-byes. I wasn't ready to say them.

As a psychologist, I worked with many patients, helping them to cope with the loss of a loved one. But suddenly, I was no longer the doctor. A profound shift in my understanding of life occurred as my eyes opened to a new world of suffering. I walked around in darkness for a while and eventually came to a crossroads. I realized I had a choice: I could run from grief or embrace it with all of its lessons. I could choose hopelessness or a life of meaning.

I chose life and meaning. That meant first embracing my grief. It wasn't easy, but unexpected things happened as I struggled through my loss. I began to feel hope again as I shared my story with others, and as others shared their stories with me. I realized just how short and precious life really is, and how much of life I had taken for granted (everything). With each passing day, I became filled with a greater sense of peace and gratitude. And as I began to make sense of the past and of my life, I began to feel a deeper sense of meaning and purpose.

Grief transformed me.

From this struggle, this book was born. Through writing it, I wish to share all that I have learned through my work as a clinician and during my own grieving process—the experiences that moved me toward greater love, gratitude, and meaning.

Although grief is painful, we can experience it as a positive, life-changing journey. We can heal from our devastation, shock, fear, and despair, and return to life again, only this time more fiercely, vulnerably, and wholeheartedly—more connected to the love that surrounds us.

There is no one right way to grieve, but how we choose to respond to loss can make the difference in living a life of bitterness or one of greater understanding, meaning, and wisdom. Grief can either ruin or mature us.

In this book, we will discuss healthy strategies to heal from the grief and devastation that results from losing a loved one, whether through a difficult death, divorce, or a breakup. Although these experiences are different, each brings its own kind of grief and pain. Our focus will be on how to live with loss interwoven in our daily lives, and how we can use our grief to transform our lives to ones filled with greater purpose, meaning, and love.

If you are in the midst of grieving the loss of a loved one, this book provides effective, practical methods for you to approach those difficulties in a way that can help you emerge stronger and more whole.

If you are further along in your experience with losing a loved one, and feel you're coping well, this book will help you discover new ways to face grief and experience deeper levels of health and fulfillment.

Although painful, the grief resulting from the loss of a loved one can serve as a catalyst for positive change and inner growth. Through grief, we can:

- become stronger and wiser,

- live with greater presence, intention, and meaning,

- love more deeply, filled with gratitude, and

- use our loss for a greater, higher purpose.

Our journeys through life, love, and loss are unique and personal, but it is my hope this book can give you some comfort or companionship along the way. Each chapter in this book addresses difficulties in the grieving process and offers specific, actionable methods for coping. This book is designed to be read through first in its entirety, and then actively turned to whenever needed over time.

As you read this book, know that the loss of a loved one is not the end. Instead, it is an opportunity to pause and reflect on your life, who you are, and where you want to be.

Know too that you are not alone in this. Together, let us resolve to take this experience of grief, with all its pain, heartbreak, and sorrow, and use it for good in our lives and of those in the world around us.

1

WHAT IS GRIEF?

Grief never ends ... but it changes. It's a passage, not a place to stay. Grief is not a sign of weakness, nor a lack of faith ... It is the price of love.

— AUTHOR UNKNOWN

$\mathcal{L}$ ove and loss are inevitable parts of life. Just as seasons change, the landscapes of our lives change, too.

We all grieve and experience intense emotional pain and heartbreak, whether due to death, divorce, or the loss of a significant relationship. Although seemingly different, grief, love, and loss unite these common experiences.

But what exactly is grief? Although we all experience grief after a loss, it is not a topic discussed much by society. Intellectually, we may know that grief is the natural response to losing someone we love—a response that involves deep sorrow, pain, and suffering—

but generally, we will not truly understand it until we experience it ourselves.

In my own personal experience grieving the loss of my marriage, many of the books I read recommended that a person should get past it, break all connection, and not look back. But I struggled to connect with this approach. And privately, I wondered if something was wrong with me. Why did I feel the loss so profoundly? Why was it so difficult to recover?

We all respond differently to loss. Some people are able to recover relatively easily from the loss of a loved one. Research has even found that some people may not grieve at all, and this is also a natural response.

Other people find it more difficult to recover. For them, the loss of someone is absolutely devastating, and they feel it profoundly.

I fell into this latter group when going through my divorce. We had built something special over the years, so I was sad that it was now gone. I needed to mourn the loss. There was no easy way to get over the pain: it was just there. There was no way to get *over* it. I needed to get *through* it.

The trouble, I soon discovered, was how to get through it without drowning in it.

This was a reflective time for me. As a clinical psychologist, I had spent a lot of time sitting with the emotional pain of others, but never really with my own. And as a first-generation Chinese-American, it would be an understatement to say that I was raised to go to great lengths to avoid any and all emotion.

It is no surprise then that I really didn't have a word for what I was experiencing—that is, until one day, when I began to read a book on grief and loss. It was for women whose spouses had died. My spouse had certainly not died, but my marriage had.

Reading that book, I realized I was not experiencing any one thing like sadness, guilt, or fear, but somehow, all of those things at once—in a word: *grief*.

And I remember experiencing incredible relief in that moment, to finally have a word for it, to finally be able to articulate what I was experiencing. After all, the first step toward healing is understanding what it is we are dealing with. After that comes hope as our loss is acknowledged by ourselves and others, and we realize we are not alone.

RECOGNIZING GRIEF

It can be difficult to realize that what we are experiencing is grief. In its most intense form, grief is most often associated with the death of a loved one. However, any loss can cause grief—the loss of a lover, a partner, time with children, friends, family, plans and dreams for the future—even if the loss was anticipated, or, in the cases of some divorces and breakups, wanted. Grief and loss are very real, no matter what the cause. Unfortunately, grief can often go unacknowledged, with many people overlooking the grief central to losing a loved one.

What also makes it difficult to identify grief is that it is a highly individual experience. It is neither a neat procession through predictable stages nor an orderly response to events. Some people may find the death of a loved one more devastating than the end of a marriage. Others may be able to recover from the death of a loved one, but be haunted by the end of a marriage or relationship breakup. We may expect to grieve some events, but not others. Some events may even catch us by surprise, complicating our response to that loss.

Indeed, grief is messy, particularly when we have lost a significant person from our lives, as this often comes with much uncertainty. Widows face an unknown future alone. Divorcees may hold out hope for reconciliation until the papers are final. The jilted partner in a romantic relationship may receive mixed signals from the one who left and could be fearful that grieving would mean the relationship is actually over. All this uncertainty when we are faced with the loss of a loved one can delay, interrupt, intensify, or prolong our feelings of grief.

THE EMOTIONAL TERRAIN OF GRIEF

One of the things that makes grief so challenging to navigate is that it is filled with unfamiliar terrain and emotion.

Although we all experience grief differently, many of us experience a range of emotions after losing a loved one. One day, we may feel devastated as we are reminded of past memories. Another day, we may feel shocked and numb, unable to comprehend what has happened. Some days, we may feel terrified as we face a future alone. And other days, we may feel angry that this has happened to us, resentful that there are others in the world so innocently unaware.

This roller coaster of emotion is normal. As such, it is natural to experience the following emotions when grieving:

Shock

Shock is our body's way of protecting us from pain—a gift of temporary anesthesia keeping us on autopilot when we are suddenly faced with loss. We find ourselves walking numbly in a fog. The unimaginable has occurred, and we are in disbelief, unable to comprehend our new reality. It feels as if we are observing life from a distance. Reality has not yet sunk in.

Sadness

When we are sad, life feels empty. It is as if we are existing in a void. Loss has shattered our lives and occupies much of our attention, making it difficult to concentrate. We may feel hopeless and wonder how we can go on. It is hard to imagine that we can ever be whole again. We feel broken, and it is all we can do to breathe.

Anger

Anger may arise abruptly and without warning. We may feel angry with the person we lost or at well-intentioned family members, friends, or strangers who try to comfort us. Sometimes, we may feel angry at life itself, or at God, for allowing us to lose our loved one. The force of our anger may surprise us.

Guilt

Guilt is a strong emotion that occurs when we consider different actions we could have taken or not taken to prevent the loss of our love. Reminded of things we regret saying and of past actions we would like to take back, we think of the different ways we feel we have failed.

Fear

Facing a strange, new world, we feel terrified. We have lost our identity and our central understanding of the world. We feel uncertain about what the future will hold and of facing life and our responsibilities alone without our partner.

Yearning

There is a deep longing for our loved one to be with us. We want to see their smile, hear their laugh, and feel their arms around us again. We continue to look for them in our lives, hoping to be in their presence once more.

Loneliness

Loneliness brings its own kind of pain. We miss the person we have lost. We ache for their companionship and the feeling of belonging we had when we were with them. We feel alone in the world. It feels as if no one understands or knows what to say to us.

PHYSICAL AND COGNITIVE SYMPTOMS OF GRIEF

As emotions are connected to the body and mind, when we are faced with loss, we may also experience physical symptoms, such as fatigue, nausea, aches and pains, difficulty sleeping, night-mares, a weakened immune system, increased blood pressure and risk of heart attack, and changes in appetite.

Changes in our thought patterns may also occur, such as increased negative thinking, inability to concentrate, indecisive-ness, overthinking, preoccupation with memories of the loved one, slower mental processing, and rumination on the past.

Thus, when experiencing a significant loss, the impact may not only be emotional, but physical and cognitive as well.

THE NATURE OF GRIEF AND LOSS

As a young psychologist, one of the first things I learned was that an emotion is not simply just an emotion; it is also the *intensity* and the *frequency* with which it is experienced, and the way in which it affects our daily lives.

Like a painting with beautifully subtle shifts and gradations, emotion colors our lives. There are few times in life when this is truer than after losing someone you love.

Relentlessness

The emotions of grief are relentless. Although the ache may dull with time, the pain of loss is always there.

John Irving illustrates this feeling in his novel *A Prayer for Owen Meany*:

> When someone you love dies, and you're not expecting it, you don't lose her all at once; you lose her in pieces over a long time —the way the mail stops coming, and her scent fades from the pillows and even from the clothes in her closet and drawers. Gradually, you accumulate the parts of her that are gone. Just when the day comes—when there's a particular missing part that overwhelms you with the feeling that she's gone, forever— there comes another day, and another specifically missing part.

Of the grief he felt during his wife's passing, writer C.S. Lewis wrote, "It doesn't really matter whether you grip the arms of the dentist's chair or let your hands lie in your lap. The drill drills on."

Waves of Intensity

Grief comes in waves, subsiding and recurring in frequency and intensity over time.

Below is a beautiful passage about this, written by a commenter on *Reddit*, a social news and discussion website. Several commenters responded to a woman seeking advice on grief ("My friend just died. I don't know what to do"), but it was the following post by G. Snow that became a classic widely shared post on grief:

> Alright, here goes. I'm old. What that means is that I've survived (so far) and a lot of people I've known and loved did not. I've lost friends, best friends, acquaintances, co-workers, grandparents, mom, relatives, teachers, mentors, students, neighbors, and a

host of other folks. I have no children, and I can't imagine the pain it must be to lose a child. But here's my two cents.

I wish I could say you get used to people dying. I never did. I don't want to. It tears a hole through me whenever somebody I love dies, no matter the circumstances. But I don't want it to "not matter." I don't want it to be something that just passes. My scars are a testament to the love and the relationship that I had for and with that person. And if the scar is deep, so was the love. So be it. Scars are a testament to life. Scars are a testament that I can love deeply and live deeply and be cut, or even gouged, and that I can heal and continue to live and continue to love. And the scar tissue is stronger than the original flesh ever was. Scars are a testament to life. Scars are only ugly to people who can't see.

As for grief, you'll find it comes in waves. When the ship is first wrecked, you're drowning, with wreckage all around you. Everything floating around you reminds you of the beauty and the magnificence of the ship that was, and is no more. And all you can do is float. You find some piece of the wreckage and you hang on for a while. Maybe it's some physical thing. Maybe it's a happy memory or a photograph. Maybe it's a person who is also floating. For a while, all you can do is float. Stay alive.

In the beginning, the waves are 100 feet tall and crash over you without mercy. They come 10 seconds apart and don't even give you time to catch your breath. All you can do is hang on and float. After a while, maybe weeks, maybe months, you'll find the waves are still 100 feet tall, but they come further apart. When they come, they still crash all over you and wipe you out. But in between, you can breathe, you can function. You never know what's going to trigger the grief. It might be a song, a picture, a street intersection, the smell of a cup of coffee. It can be just about anything ... and the wave comes crashing. But in between waves, there is life.

Somewhere down the line, and it's different for everybody, you find that the waves are only 80 feet tall. Or 50 feet tall. And while they still come, they come further apart. You can see them coming. An anniversary, a birthday, or Christmas, or landing at O'Hare. You can see it coming, for the most part, and prepare yourself. And when it washes over you, you know that somehow you will, again, come out the other side. Soaking wet, sputtering, still hanging on to some tiny piece of the wreckage, but you'll come out ...

Profound Losses

The impact of losing someone you love is profound, with both immediate and gradual effects that ripple across time. With any major loss come many other losses—the loss of our identity, companionship, financial security, and shared plans for the future—each seemingly small, but sometimes equally as devastating.

STAGES OF GRIEF

The Kübler-Ross model proposes that most people typically progress through five different stages of grief when healing from a loss: *denial, anger, bargaining, depression, and acceptance.*

This model, developed by Elisabeth Kübler-Ross in 1969, has been helpful in providing a framework for thinking about grief, but research now indicates that there is no linear progression through "stages" when faced with loss.

Instead, the latest science suggests that although denial, anger, bargaining, depression, and acceptance are *emotions* felt when experiencing loss, there is no one typical pattern of grief response. The experience of grief is as varied and as unique as our losses. It is a journey that everyone goes through differently. Thus, there is no final acceptance stage of grief, but rather, a continuous process of adjusting and learning to live with our loss and our new reality.

PATTERNS OF GRIEF

Psychologist George Bonanno conducted intensive studies in which he followed thousands of people over long periods of time to study how they responded to loss and traumatic events such as divorce or the death of a spouse. Through this work, he discovered several different grief patterns.

Some people experience a prolonged and enduring grief, struggling for years to recover from the loss of their loved one. In fact, over time, their grief worsens.

Other people experience intense grief, but gradually begin to recover. They never forget the loss but eventually learn to live with the loss in a healthy manner.

But Dr. Bonanno found something startling in his work: most people demonstrate great resilience in the face of loss. They experience an intense, acute period of sadness, which then begins to subside. The loss deeply affects them, but they are able to recover and continue facing the daily demands of life. Although they experience moments of sadness that come and go, they also experience moments of laughter and joy as healthy and protective responses to loss.

This work has profound implications for how we think about loss and the healing process. In it, we see that, although grief is very painful, it can eventually give rise to renewed hope. We also see that resilience is not something unobtainable. Rather, many who experience loss show a surprising capacity for it. After losing someone we love, we *can* recover. Though forever changed in fundamental ways, we can find ways to face the future.

Tears shed for another person are not a sign of weakness. They are a sign of a pure heart.

— JOSÉ N. HARRIS

2

EMBRACE GRIEF AND VULNERABILITY

Owning our story can be hard but not nearly as difficult as spending our lives running from it. Embracing our vulnerabilities is risky but not nearly as dangerous as giving up on love and belonging and joy— the experiences that make us the most vulnerable. Only when we are brave enough to explore the darkness will we discover the infinite power of our light.

— BRENÉ BROWN

*W*hen we lose someone we love, we feel raw and helpless. Emotions well up within us without warning. We see reminders of our loved one everywhere—in the lines of a song, in the empty pillow beside us, in the books they loved to read—and are overwhelmed with grief. We remember all we have lost and come face-to-face with our vulnerability.

There are many different ways of coping with the loss of a loved one. Although there is no "right" way to grieve, some coping styles are healthier and more life affirming than others.

Faced with the difficult emotions of grief, many of us may want to run from them and push them away. Others of us may be in shock or denial or stoically feel we must be strong for others. It makes sense. Given the significance of what we are faced with, it is only natural that we would want to numb ourselves or suppress our pain.

While training to become a psychologist, I worked with Catherine, a young woman who had lost her husband, Kevin, in a tragic motor vehicle accident. Kevin had been a few years older, and they had grown up together as best friends. Prior to his death, they had been planning to have a baby. They were trying to conceive and had recently purchased a new home for their future family. They had even come up with a list of potential baby names.

But these plans never happened. Catherine's whole life had changed in an instant.

Catherine had never envisioned a life without Kevin, so she struggled to sleep, and cried all the time. She often found herself searching for Kevin without thinking, half expecting to see him wherever she looked.

Her family tried to help her by saying that Kevin was in a better place, and that death happens to everyone. Her friends did not know what to say and so said nothing at all.

Catherine felt very alone.

Without Kevin, Catherine confessed to her sister, she felt as if she had nothing more to live for. Her family became concerned for her wellbeing, and so she agreed to seek help and support.

Together, Catherine and I worked on developing strategies to help her sit with her pain. Rather than suppressing or resisting her emotions, she learned to experience them without judgment, to allow her emotions to flow and to surrender to her feelings of grief and loss.

With time, Catherine began to make progress: she began sleeping better, reconnecting with friends and family, and returning to her hobbies of writing and hiking. She realized that life would never be the same but that she could learn a new way to live—a different life, but one nevertheless shaped by her time and experiences with Kevin. As Catherine embraced her pain, something shifted inside her, and she began to live each day with a new sense of gratitude.

Faced with the difficult emotions of grief and loss, it is natural to want to avoid them. But this form of coping is unhealthy, as the avoidance of pain only serves to intensify it and to give it greater power over us. Although counterintuitive, when we open ourselves to feeling the emotions of grief, we also leave our hearts open to healing.

HOW TO EMBRACE GRIEF

Grief is a natural and healthy response to loss. What if we invited it in and welcomed it instead of resisting? Yes, it is painful, but oftentimes struggling against pain only causes more suffering. So, what if we allowed ourselves to feel and experience it?

Grief is an invitation to honor our loss—to develop greater emotional resilience and strength. It is an invitation to transform the pain we are carrying into greater peace, meaning, and joy, so that ultimately, we can heal.

It's okay to feel pain and to become intimate with it—that's where healing begins. This chapter describes several different ways to embrace grief. Try these techniques out and see which methods connect the most with you personally.

eel Your Emotions

There is a sacredness in tears. They are not the mark of weakness, but of power. They speak more eloquently than ten thousand tongues. They are the messengers of overwhelming grief, of deep contrition, and of unspeakable love.

— WASHINGTON IRVING

Grief is a sign that you loved deeply. It will take time for the sadness to ease and for you to develop a new sense of normalcy. Others may make you feel as if you should speed up your grieving process. Ignore them. Allow yourself to grieve at your own pace, to turn inward, and for grief to unfold in a way that is natural for you.

To get in touch with your emotions, you can try the following:

- NOTICE AND LABEL YOUR EMOTIONS: When you feel an emotion, name it to yourself. For example: "I'm feeling sad right now." This will help you become more in touch with your emotions.

- MONITOR YOUR EMOTIONS: Pay attention to how you are feeling throughout the day. When you feel a particular emotion, record it into a journal or a mood-tracking app. One app that is particularly helpful is iMood Journal. It helps you record how you are feeling along with the things that you think are affecting your mood, like sleep troubles, anxiety, stress, or positive things, like a kind thing someone said. It then charts patterns of your moods over time, so you can better understand things that improve or worsen your mood.

pen Your Heart to Discomfort

"What happens when people open their hearts"?

"They get better."

— HARUKI MURAKAMI, NORWEGIAN WOOD

Losing someone you love can leave you feeling vulnerable, unwanted, or even abandoned. Your natural inclination may be to protect yourself from being hurt—to shut down and put on heavy emotional armor. But the problem is that shielding yourself from vulnerability may also shield you from love, connection, meaning, and peace. Closing yourself off to negative emotions also closes you to positive ones. Therefore, vulnerability is an important key to healing.

To be vulnerable, allow yourself to feel discomfort. Examples include:

- being alone rather than rushing into a new relationship.

- doing something for the first time that your partner used to do (like cooking).

- telling your friends and family how you are feeling.

Sometimes discomfort is a sign that we are where we need to be. So step into that uncertainty. Welcome all feelings with a gentle curiosity. Greet fears with an open heart.

ultivate Mindfulness

Mindfulness means paying attention in a particular way: On purpose, in the present moment, and nonjudgmentally.

— JON KABAT-ZINN

Practicing mindfulness meditation can help you to relieve stress and suffering as you stay focused on the present moment.

When our minds are stuck in the past, our feelings of loss are intensified. Similarly, when our thoughts are focused on the future, we tend to become anxious and worried.

Staying focused on the present doesn't mean we forget about the past or don't think about the future. It just means we don't keep our minds there. We remain present, in the here and now, open to the emotions of grief and the insight that it brings.

Through meditation, we connect to the timeless wisdom within us. With tenderness, patience, and compassion, it opens our hearts to the present moment, allowing us to feel gratitude and joy.

There are many simple ways to meditate and practice mindfulness:

- DEEP BREATHING: Sit comfortably and pay attention to your breath. As you breathe, let go of everything —all the tension, grief, and stress—and breathe it

out. When your attention wanders, return to your
breath.

- PAY ATTENTION TO YOUR SENSES: Take a flower and
  perceive every detail of it—its colors, textures, shape,
  and scent. Notice how connected you feel to this simple
  object and moment.

- OBSERVE YOUR THOUGHTS AND EMOTIONS: Close your eyes
  and visualize a gently flowing stream with leaves floating
  along the surface of the water. Take all your thoughts
  and emotions that form and simply place each of them
  on a leaf and let them float by. Do the same for any
  thoughts that come up during this practice. Exercises
  like this can help you recognize that you are not your
  thoughts. Thoughts are just thoughts, not necessarily
  true, as transient as leaves on a stream.

- ACCEPT YOUR EMOTIONS AS THEY ARE, WITHOUT
  JUDGMENT: Our minds have a natural tendency to judge
  our emotions. We may feel bad and then feel bad about
  feeling bad, thus feeling even worse. So, whatever
  emotions you are feeling, try to resist fighting, escaping,
  or struggling against them. Instead, relax and let your
  emotions come as they will, and accept them without
  judgment.

There is a great peace that can be found through meditation. If
you are interested in learning more, check out the following
resources:

BOOKS

- *The Miracle of Mindfulness: An Introduction to the Practice of Meditation* by **Thich Nhat Hanh.** Offers gentle, practical advice for learning the skills of mindfulness. Here is one of my favorite quotes from this essential book: "People usually consider walking on water or in thin air a miracle. But I think the real miracle is not to walk either on water or in thin air, but to walk on earth. Every day we are engaged in a miracle which we don't even recognize: a blue sky, white clouds, green leaves, the black, curious eyes of a child—our own two eyes. All is a miracle."

- *Grieving Mindfully: A Compassion and Spiritual Guide to Coping with Loss* by **Sameet M. Kumar, PhD.** Provides information on how to apply mindfulness to cope with grieving. Here's one of my favorite observations from this book: "Grief is not an identity. What feels so solid and real as a grief reaction (or any other reaction) in any moment is merely a combination of powerful reactive habits of thinking, feeling, and physical sensations."

WEBSITES

- *ChopraCenterMeditation.com*: Hosts a range of free meditations that vary in style.

APPS

- **Headspace:** Guided and unguided mediations varying in length of time.

- **Insight Timer:** Free guided meditations where you can meet others in the world who are meditating with you.

Take One Step at a Time

The man who removes a mountain begins by carrying away small stones.

— CHINESE PROVERB

The thought of making it through weeks, months, and even years without your loved one can be overwhelming. Know that you don't have to tackle everything at once. It's okay to face things one day at a time. Focus on specifics. For example, what will you eat today? What work do you need to do today? Allow yourself to focus on each moment and each day as it comes.

Not only can we face things one day at a time, but we can also tackle tasks one step at a time to make them more manageable. For example, one of my clients felt overwhelmed when faced with filing taxes on her own for the first time following her divorce. We worked together to break this large task into smaller steps:

- Purchasing tax preparation software

- Creating a special folder for tax documents

- Identifying the different sources she needed tax documents from

- Collecting tax documents into the folder

- Reading about tax questions online (fifteen minutes per day for three to four days)

- Entering basic information into the tax preparation software

- Filling out the tax form one section at a time

By breaking down this large task into smaller, more manageable steps, she was able to effectively tackle something intimidating during a difficult time in her life. Using this strategy helped her feel calmer and less overwhelmed, and reduced her feelings of stress.

*E*stablish Daily Routines

Grief is in two parts. The first is loss. The second is the remaking of life.

— ANNE ROIPHE

Grief and loss can disrupt many areas of life, contributing to increased stress and chaos. A routine can help you maintain a sense of structure, normalcy, and security, helping you feel more grounded and centered.

Naturally, there will be times when you do not feel like doing any of your normal activities, such as getting out of bed or going to work. However, after you have taken some time off to grieve your loss, it is healthiest to resume your typical routine: to hold grief in one hand while you take on life with the other.

For example, even if you are still experiencing feelings of grief, continue to:

- do household tasks

- eat regular meals

- pay the bills

- go to work

- take time for self-care

- exercise

- spend time with family and friends

You may not feel like doing any of these things at first, but stick with it and you will gradually begin to feel better.

If you are having trouble feeling motivated to do an activity, it can help to reduce the friction associated with that activity or task in order to make it easier to accomplish. For instance, if the activity is to do the dishes, you could tell yourself that you will wash two dishes in the sink. But by the time you have washed those two dishes, you may feel okay washing the rest since you are already at the sink anyway.

*L*earn the Differences Between Normal Grief, Depression, and Complicated Grief

Her absence is like the sky, spread over everything.

— C. S. LEWIS, A GRIEF OBSERVED

While it is healthy to embrace grief, there is a point where you may feel grief so intensely and frequently that it becomes unhealthy and affects your daily functioning. Thus, it can be helpful for you to understand the distinctions between normal grief, depression, and complicated grief, so you can seek extra support.

- GRIEF: Grief involves a myriad of emotions—both negative and positive—that may be felt on different days and at different times. The predominant feeling of grief is often one of emptiness and loss. With time, grief will begin to lift.

- DEPRESSION: Depression is more constant and is primarily characterized by sustained melancholy or inability to experience pleasure. Symptoms include difficulty carrying out responsibilities and tasks in different areas of life, thoughts of death or suicide, feelings of intense guilt, and constant thoughts of worthlessness or hopelessness.

- COMPLICATED GRIEF: When intense grief persists and is so severe and prolonged that it is disabling and interferes with one's life long after the loss, it is known as complicated grief. Symptoms include strong avoidance of reminders of the loved one, intrusive thoughts about the loss that disrupt daily activities, recurrent distressing emotions, feelings that life without the loved one has no meaning, and a desire to rejoin the loved one (in the case of death, through suicide).

If you feel that you are experiencing depression or complicated grief, speak with a mental health professional. Losing someone you love is one of the most difficult things you will ever face, so it is only natural to get extra support during this time.

Make a Choice

Grief is like the ocean; it comes on waves ebbing and flowing. Sometimes the water is calm, and sometimes it is overwhelming. All we can do is learn to swim.

— VICKI HARRISON

It may take time for the emotions of grief and loss to subside, but in the meantime, you can actively engage in actions to begin healing. Though you did not have much control over this experience of loss, you do have control over how you wish to respond to that loss in order to create the life you want. Sheryl Sandberg, chief operating officer of Facebook, wrote about this feeling a month after her husband, David Goldberg, died:

> I think when tragedy occurs, it presents a choice. You can give in to the void, the emptiness that fills your heart, your lungs, constricts your ability to think or even breathe. Or you can try to find meaning. These past thirty days, I have spent many of my moments lost in that void. And I know that many future moments will be consumed by the vast emptiness as well. But when I can, I want to choose life and meaning.

Although it may seem counterintuitive, when we allow room in our lives for grief, healing can occur. So allow yourself to feel your emotions, to be vulnerable. Meditate. Continue your daily routines and take things one step and one day at a time. Embrace grief. Choose life and meaning.

Grief can be the garden of compassion. If you keep your heart open through everything, your pain can become your greatest ally in your life's search for love and wisdom.

— RUMI

3

CULTIVATE CONNECTION

Deep grief sometimes is almost like a specific location, a coordinate on a map of time. When you are standing in that forest of sorrow, you cannot imagine that you could ever find your way to a better place. But if someone can assure you that they themselves have stood in that same place, and now have moved on, sometimes this will bring hope.

— ELIZABETH GILBERT, EAT, PRAY, LOVE

*L*osing someone you loved can make you feel very lonely. Perhaps they knew you in a special way, and now it feels like that part of your life is irretrievably lost. You had a unique history together, filled with good times and bad times, common memories and critical experiences that only the two of you shared.

Perhaps this person was not only your partner, but also your best friend, lover, and primary source of emotional support and advice. Your connection to certain friends. Your family accountant, personal chef, driver, and everything else in between. Humor once filled your shared life with laughter, and now there is only deep silence as you struggle alone with your loss of that person. Everything that was familiar is now gone, and the person you need to help you get through it is no longer here.

It may be hard for others to understand what you are going through. Or they may think they understand, but they really don't. This may make us keep to ourselves, afraid to burden others, feeling as if they may not be able to handle our pain.

It can be shocking to realize that someone you love will not be in your life again, even if the loss is anticipated over time. My friend Nora, whose husband died of stage 4 colon cancer, explained:

> The doctors told us that my husband had stage 4 colon cancer and that he had about a year to live. He did, in fact, die one year later. During that year we had plenty of time to say all that needed to be said, but it was both heartbreaking and shocking to come home from the hospital, get into bed, and know that I'd never have him next to me again.

She spoke of how important the support of others was to her during that isolating, lonely time:

> The first few months after his death ... I realized that my life was pretty empty. During the ten years I was married to him, I had neglected to keep in touch with most of my friends ... Recognizing how lonely I was, I decided to reach out to my women friends to spend time with them again. I also contacted my college roommate, who was living in another state ... I even got to know my next-door neighbor, whom I had barely known except to say hi to from my driveway.

Coincidentally, it was she who introduced me to the person who would become my second husband. Even as I was getting to know this person I would eventually marry, I continued to grieve for the partner I had lost. It was a difficult balance, but one that I was able to navigate with the help of psychotherapy, a widows' support group, and, perhaps most importantly, my friends.

Spending time with friends who cared about me was extremely important in my grieving process. Besides feeling supported by them, it was valuable to have events on my calendar—places I needed to be and people who expected me to be there. I was able to step out of my own pain for a while and provide support to others who had challenges of their own.

Nora's story is a hopeful reminder that, although it may feel like it, the loss of a loved one is not the end. Instead, it is an opportunity to reassemble the pieces of our lives—to get to know ourselves in new and different ways. The hole of our loss will never be filled, but with the help of others, life can begin to take root.

One of my patients, Becky, had split up with her boyfriend of ten years. For days afterward, she said she felt as if life was passing her by like scenery through a car window. She'd look at laughing couples at the park, wondering how it was that others could be so happy. This was a different type of loneliness, she said, one of disconnection—a loneliness beyond loneliness. Gradually, that feeling went away, but it took time. She said what helped her the most was the presence of family and friends simply being with her as she navigated this new, unfamiliar world after loss.

HOW TO CULTIVATE CONNECTION

Loss can sometimes cause us to feel incredibly lonely. We realize that, despite all the people in our lives, we must ultimately travel through life alone. And the thought of this fills us with intense despair.

To overcome these feelings of loneliness, it helps to connect with others. When we do this, we no longer feel alone. We exchange shared experiences and stories of loss and suffering, and somehow, pain and misery become easier to bear. We know this at a personal level, but research also supports this, indicating that social support is strongly related to greater resilience and healing after traumatic events and losses.

Here are some simple ways to cultivate connection with others when you are feeling alone:

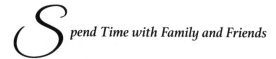

Spend Time with Family and Friends

Don't walk behind me; I may not lead. Don't walk in front of me; I may not follow. Just walk beside me and be my friend.

— ALBERT CAMUS

Turn towards supportive friends and family members and spend time with them. Let them know that they do not need to have the answers, but that it helps just to have someone to listen.

Sometimes people have good intentions but come across as critical or judgmental. It's okay to distance yourself from these unhelpful people during your healing process.

Focus instead on surrounding yourself with people who are supportive, positive, and hopeful—people with whom you can be open about what you are going through.

 *pen Up*

The closest bonds we will ever know are bonds of grief. The deepest community one of sorrow.

— CORMAC MCCARTHY, ALL THE PRETTY
HORSES

Be open about what you're going through, allowing others to see you as you really are and the struggles you are facing. This can help you feel cared for and understood as your loss is acknowledged.

Letting others know what you are going through may also lead them to share their own experiences with you, which may bring you greater comfort and hope. As you reflect on your own struggles and vulnerability, you will develop a deeper understanding and empathy for others. This will also help you feel supported, thus decreasing your feelings of loneliness.

There are different ways to tell others how you are feeling:

- SHARE HOW YOU FEEL: Begin with this phrase: "I'm feeling ..." Then, say what emotion you are currently feeling. For example, "I'm feeling sad." "I'm feeling angry." It can also help to name the cause of your emotion, such as, "I'm feeling sad because it would have been our anniversary today."

- BE VULNERABLE: Opening up to others means being vulnerable (see Chapter 1). After the loss of my marriage, I'd sometimes admit to my friends that, "Yes, I'm having a really difficult time right now, and I have been feeling really lost lately." And I was often surprised by how

supportive they were, and how touched I felt, knowing
that when I cried there was someone crying along
with me.

- SET LIMITS: You may find there are times when you don't
  feel comfortable sharing or when the loss is too painful
  to talk about. That's okay. It's healthy to set limits and
  acknowledge when you do and do not feel comfortable
  sharing with others.

- EXPRESS YOUR LOVE: Love is the highest and ultimate
  way to connect with others. You can express your love in
  many simple ways, such as a hug, a touch, spending time
  with the person you love, or doing something thoughtful
  for them.

*A*sk for Help

Some things in life cannot be fixed. They can only be carried.

— MEGAN DEVINE

The people in your life very likely want to help you but do not
know how. Tell them specifically what you need and how they
can best help you. It's good to be assertive. People will feel
grateful to know how best to support you.

Examples of some things you could ask for include:

- someone to listen

- a lunch or dinner out together

- someone to go on a walk with

- childcare

- pet care

- help with cooking meals

- grocery shopping

- laundry

 *ultivate New Friendships:*

Friendship improves happiness and abates misery, by the doubling of our joy and the dividing of our grief.

— MARCUS TULLIUS CICER

In certain cases, you may have lost not only your loved one, but your main support system as well, such as shared friends and family you were primarily connected to through your loved one. If this is the case, spend time developing new friendships. Find others with shared interests, hobbies, or passions so you can find a common ground, making it easier to connect. Some places you could try exploring include:

- SPECIAL INTEREST GROUPS: *Meetup.com* is a great website where you can find groups of people who share similar interests as well as organized events related to hiking, book clubs, dinner clubs, triathlon training, and much more.

- CLASSES: Take classes in an area that interests you, such as cooking, photography, knitting, spinning, or yoga.

- PLACES OF WORSHIP: Places of worship can also be a great place to find community and people with similar interests and beliefs. Look up local places of worship around your area and attend a service. Some may have a welcome team to welcome you, or you may meet others who are attending for the first time.

- ATTEND LOCAL EVENTS: Gallery openings, festivals and fairs, music concerts, art shows, and book readings are all great places to meet people with similar interests. *Yelp.com* is one such website that lists upcoming local events.

ind a Support Group

I would rather walk with a friend in the dark, than alone in the light.

— HELEN KELLER

Sometimes it can be helpful to attend support groups to connect with others who are have also experienced loss. Members can offer comfort, encouragement, connection, and suggestions, all which help you feel less alone. You can find different support groups at counseling centers, hospitals, and places of worship, or online resources such as:

- *Meetup.com*: A website that lists various groups of people you can meet up with, including those who are going through breakups, divorces, or loss of a partner through death or illness.

- *GriefShare.org*: Support for people grieving the death of a loved one.

- **American Foundation for Suicide Prevention (AFSP.org):** Support for suicide survivors.

- *Facebook.com*: If you don't have time to attend a local support group, you can find and join support groups for grief, divorce, and breakups on Facebook.

iscover Comforting Books

Books are the quietest and most constant of friends; they are the most accessible and wisest of counsellors, and the most patient of teachers.

— CHARLES WILLIAM ELIOT

Books can provide great wisdom and advice and help us feel we are not alone. Reading memoirs or books that talk about others who have gone through the same thing can help us feel as if there are people we can relate to who have been there and survived.

Here are a few books about loss and love that may help you feel less alone:

- *The Year of Magical Thinking* by **Joan Didion.** This

memoir describes the author's journey through grief after the death of her husband.

- *Option B: Facing Adversity, Building Resilience, and Finding Joy* by **Sheryl Sandberg.** Helpful and moving book written by the chief operating officer of Facebook about dealing with the sudden passing of her husband.

- *A Grief Observed* by **C. S. Lewis.** A very honest book C.S. Lewis wrote after his wife passed away. In it, he grapples with fundamental questions about loss, faith, and the meaning of life.

- *Tuesdays with Morrie: An Old Man, A Young Man, and Life's Greatest Lesson* by **Mitch Albom.** Inspirational true story in which the author reconnects with his university professor, Morrie, as he is nearing the end of his life. Full of helpful life lessons and wisdom.

- *Tiny, Beautiful Things: Advice on Love and Life from Dear Sugar* by **Cheryl Strayed.** A book of letters from the author's anonymous advice column. A compassionate book that reminds us we are not alone in our pain.

- *The Sky is Everywhere* by **Jandy Nelson.** This beautifully written fictional story of seventeen-year-old Lennie Walker, whose sister suddenly dies, is full of emotion as Lennie works through the complicated truths of heartbreak and loss. Here's one of my favorite quotes from this book: "Grief and love are conjoined, you don't get one without the other. All I can do is love her, and love the world, emulate her by living with daring and spirit and joy."

- *Good Grief* by Granger E. Westberg. A short, comforting book on finding hope and comfort through grief and loss. The author reminds us that grief is natural and felt for any type of loss in life.

- *Healing After Loss: Daily Meditations for Working Through Grief* by Martha W. Hickman. Daily quotes and meditations for anyone who has suffered the loss of a loved one. Compassionate, comforting, and healing.

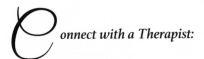 *onnect with a Therapist:*

You can't stay in your corner of the Forest waiting for others to come to you. You have to go to them sometimes.

— A.A. MILNE, WINNIE-THE-POOH

Many people find working with a therapist helpful during this challenging time. Therapists can help you work through your grief and through the barriers to your healing. If your grief has progressed into depression or complicated grief, seeing a therapist can be crucial.

If you are interested in finding a therapist, you can try the following resources:

- *Psychology Today.com*: This website has a comprehensive directory of therapists and customized search features based on insurance plan, location, and therapy type.

- **FindCBT.org:** Find a therapist that practices Cognitive Behavioral Therapy (CBT), widely considered to be the gold standard treatment for psychotherapy. Search by therapist specialty and insurance plan.

- **Your local university's psychology or psychiatry department:** They may have a clinic where graduate students provide therapy at a discounted rate under the supervision of qualified, licensed professionals.

- **Your local hospital's psychology or psychiatry department:** They may have psychologists or psychiatrists on staff and covered by insurance. Or they can send you a list of suggested referrals.

Once you've found a potential therapist, try seeing them for one appointment to determine if he or she is a good fit for you.

*R*ecovering from the loss of someone you love is deeply challenging, but know that you aren't alone in this. There are others out there to comfort and share your pain during this difficult time. Connect and spend time with them. Open up and cultivate new friendships. Express your love.

The friend who can be silent with us in a moment of despair or confusion, who can stay with us in an hour of grief or bereavement, who can tolerate not knowing ... not healing, not curing ... that is a friend who cares.

— HENRI NOUWEN

4

LOVE AND NOURISH YOURSELF

The most beautiful people we have known are those who have known defeat, known suffering, known struggle, known loss, and have found their way out of the depths. These persons have an appreciation, a sensitivity and an understanding of life that fills them with compassion, gentleness, and a deep loving concern. Beautiful people do not just happen.

— ELIZABETH KÜBLER-ROSS

Some of the most difficult things about loss are all the firsts—the first time we wake up in the morning without our loved one, the first time they do not walk through the front door. Though seemingly small, each loss is devastating. And they are ongoing.

There is a whole lifetime remaining of firsts.

It is hard to rebuild a life when sometimes all we can think about is our loved one. It is hard when a memory of that person suddenly arises, and we remember all too clearly all we have lost and the life that is to be no more. Sometimes, we dwell on the mistakes we've made and the regrets of the past, and our hearts feel heavy and broken.

One of my patients, Steve, lost his wife in a swimming accident. For many months, he struggled with feelings of guilt about an argument they had just before her accident. He kept imagining scenarios in which his wife did not die. "If only I hadn't asked her to come swimming with me," he'd say. "If only I could have been more present in our last moments together."

Divorces and breakups can also bring unexpected loss when the end of the relationship is unwanted by one partner. This sudden loss can trigger feelings of abandonment, rejection, and shame. Diana, who suddenly found out her partner was cheating on her, felt as if the world was moving beneath her feet. She experienced incredible pain and was overwhelmed with feelings of guilt that she was somehow not the partner her husband needed. The betrayal brought up a lot of old emotions related to her childhood that she hadn't yet worked through, such as feelings of abandonment by her mother, who had left her as a young child with her father. So there were many layers to her loss that she needed to process and work through.

The stress of loss can leave us mentally, emotionally, physically, and spiritually depleted. Grieving takes much strength and courage. Be kind to yourself. Show yourself the kind of love and compassion you would show to a close friend who was going through something like this.

HOW TO LOVE AND NOURISH YOURSELF

It can be hard to love ourselves. After all, there is no one we spend more time with, no one we know more deeply—faults, imperfections, battle scars, and all.

When people start to love themselves, they feel happier. They feel more confident and secure. They feel a greater sense of peace and wellbeing.

Loving yourself involves having a deep appreciation for who you are. It isn't selfish. It allows you to grow in love and to give yourself more fully to others.

Here are some actions you can take today to love and get to know yourself more deeply. You don't have to try all of them at once. Choose a few to try out today, and work your way through the others at your own pace.

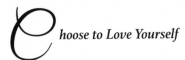

*C**hoose to Love Yourself*

> *Only people who are capable of loving strongly can also suffer great sorrow, but this same necessity of loving serves to counteract their grief and heals them.*
>
> — LEO TOLSTOY

Just as we decide to do things that will lead to feelings of anger, sadness, or other emotions, we can choose to love and treat ourselves kindly with our decisions, behaviors, and self-talk. This involves seeing yourself with eyes of love and compassion. You are worthy of love, so choose to love yourself, even with all your imperfections.

ractice Self-Compassion

This is a moment of suffering. <u>Suffering is part of life. May I be kind to myself in this moment.</u> May I give myself the compassion I need.

— KRISTEN NEFF

Self-compassion is defined as being kind, supportive, and understanding toward yourself. Rather than judging and criticizing yourself which leads to greater suffering, self-compassion involves treating yourself with warmth, love, and unconditional acceptance.

Practice self-compassion by doing the following:

- **BE KIND TO YOURSELF**

Self-compassion is simply giving the same kindness to ourselves that we would give to others.

— CHRISTOPHER GERMER

Be <u>patient and understanding with yourself</u>. You've experienced a significant loss, and it will take time to recover—and that's okay. For instance, you may not be able to be quite as productive on the job or perform at the level you are used to because you are filled with memories of your loved one and are finding it difficult to concentrate. Know that this is expected and normal.

- **TRANSFORM YOUR MINDSET**

You have been criticizing yourself for years, and it hasn't worked. Try approving of yourself and see what happens.

— LOUISE L. HAY

Your thoughts greatly influence how you feel. Words have a powerful influence on emotions and moods, so try to challenge those negative thoughts when they come, and practice some positive affirmations instead, such as:

- I am healing each day.

- I am worthy of love and joy.

- I am improving my life each day.

- I love and accept myself.

- **FORGIVE YOURSELF**

It took me a long time to learn that mistakes aren't good or bad, they're just mistakes, and you clean them up and go on.

— KAYE GIBBONS

Guilt is a natural part of grief, often surfacing as we search for an explanation for and make meaning from our loss. This can lead to feelings of doubt, shame, and unworthiness. If your loss was sudden or unexpected, you may feel heartbroken thinking about the things you did or didn't do, or the things you did or didn't say to your loved one.

Sometimes it can help to understand that your loss is the result of a chain of events that occurred even before you were born. Chances are that the loss is the result of many issues, most of which you had no control over. We're human, and it is human nature to make mistakes. Know that you did the best you could with what you knew at the time.

However, if there is something that you think you did do wrong, know that is also okay. Guilt can have a healthy aspect to it, in that it allows us to take responsibility and learn from our mistakes, but don't get lost in it. Resolve to forgive yourself, and to learn and grow from the experience. To practice forgiveness, try the following:

- Identify the thoughts that are leading to feelings of guilt. When they arise, practice mindfulness meditation (see Chapter 2).

- Consider what you can do to make amends. Make them to the extent you are able.

- Explore your spirituality to learn what God or a higher power may have to say about forgiveness.

 *alidate Yourself*

The truth is that it hurts because it's real. It hurts because it mattered. And that's an important thing to acknowledge to yourself. But that doesn't mean that it won't end, it won't get better. Because it will.

— JOHN GREEN

Maybe you are very critical of yourself. Or perhaps well-meaning people in your life have said things that are insensitive or invalidating to your suffering or pain. Perhaps they said they know how you feel, or wonder why you're not "over it already."

It's human nature to look to others for comfort or validation. It feels good to be loved and encouraged by others. But we don't need someone else's love to feel love. We don't need someone else's validation to be happy. We can love and accept ourselves.

Recognize how difficult it is to experience a loss such as this, and know that you are in the process of healing. Let all your fears, worries, and pain go. Acknowledge the loss you've experienced and the impact it's had on your life. Honor what is true to you and connect to the part of yourself that intuitively knows how to heal. Relax into this new space, trusting that in the long term, you'll be okay.

Some ways to validate your experience include:

- Picture yourself as a small child, one who just wants to be loved and heard. What would you say to a child going through this?

- What would you say if your best friend were going through this? Whatever you would tell them, tell it to yourself.

- Practice journaling and writing about the progress you've made, the struggles you are facing, and the positive decisions and choices you are proud of.

Focus on One Change at a Time

Each of us has his own rhythm of suffering.

— ROLAND BARTHES

Focus on healing from your loss and all the changes it has brought. Hold off on making any major life changes for the time being. It can be difficult to make healthy, well-informed decisions when under high amounts of stress, as your focus may be spread very thin. Give yourself a few months to a year to adjust to your loss before making any major decisions, such as changing jobs or moving. By waiting to make major decisions, your decisions will be better informed, thus minimizing stress and allowing for greater peace.

xercise

Give your stress wings, and let it fly away.

— TERRI GUILLEMETS

Exercise is healthy for your body and mind. It releases endorphins, which help with mood and stress management. However, choose a type of exercise that you are genuinely interested in, so you can stay engaged. Do anything that makes you feel good. Activities like walking, gardening, running, biking, dancing, swimming, and yoga are all forms of exercise. When you feel good physically, you will also feel good emotionally.

et Better Sleep

Nourishing yourself in a way that helps you blossom in the direction you want to go is attainable, and you are worth the effort.

— DEBORAH DAY

When we are tired and stressed, everything in life feels even harder and more difficult to cope with. Thus, during this season of grief, a healthy balance of both rest and work is essential. Make sure to take time to rest and recharge each day and to get good sleep each night. The more well-rested you are, the more you will be able to manage your emotions, cope with stress, and continue meeting your life responsibilities.

Some ways to promote good sleep include:

- Avoid caffeine four to six hours before bedtime.

- Make your bedroom dark, quiet, and cool.

- Establish a relaxing bedtime routine to transition from wakefulness to sleep, such as taking a bath, reading a book, or meditating before going to bed.

- Turn your clock away from you to avoid watching it at night.

- Go to bed and wake up at consistent times each day to help your body's internal clock know when to expect sleep.

Relax and De-stress

Sometimes the most important thing in a whole day is the rest we take between two deep breaths.

— ETTY HILLESUM

Rest doesn't just mean sleep. Relaxation is also a form of rest and can feel greatly restorative. Engage in calming and soothing activities such as getting a massage, savoring a warm cup of tea, listening to relaxing music, taking a hot bath, journaling, reading a book, or meditating.

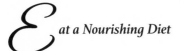

at a Nourishing Diet

It's not selfish to love yourself, take care of yourself, and to make your happiness a priority. It's necessary.

— MANDY HALE

Nutrition has been linked to emotional, physical, and cognitive health, so make sure you eat a healthy diet to give yourself the vitamins and nutrients you need to heal and stay well. Nourishing your body will also help with improved mood and energy.

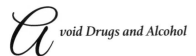

void Drugs and Alcohol

I have absolutely no pleasure in the stimulants in which I sometimes so madly indulge. It has not been in the pursuit of pleasure that I have periled life and reputation and reason. It has been the desperate attempt to escape from torturing memories, from a sense of insupportable loneliness and a dread of some strange impending doom.

— EDGAR ALLAN POE

When you're navigating difficult emotions, it can be tempting to escape from the pain by using drugs and alcohol. Try to avoid this at all costs. Substances like drugs and alcohol may offer a means of coping in the short term, but they are depressants that can intensify negative emotions and prevent you from coping with grief in a healthy way in the long term.

If your emotions are extremely difficult to cope with, or if you have a family history that places you at increased risk for substance abuse, it can be helpful to find professional mental health and emotional support. Grief can be like a dark tunnel with seemingly no end in sight, so build a network of health professionals and social supports to walk with you through to the other side.

ind Joy

When you recover or discover something that nourishes your soul and brings joy, care enough about yourself to make room for it in your life.

— JEAN SHINODA BOLEN

Carve out time for yourself each day to do things that replenish your spirit and bring you joy. At first, you may not feel interested in going out with friends or engaging in the activities you used to enjoy. This is natural. However, in the long-term, avoiding activity can lead to feeling worse over time.

Activities can include:

- drawing

- walking

- reading

- painting

- writing

- spending an evening with friends

- trying out new restaurants

- exercising

- learning new skills

- taking a day trip

- hiking

- gardening

- watching a movie

- cooking

- cleaning

- playing a musical instrument

- visiting museums and art galleries

Discover New Passions

We are each gifted in a unique and important way. It is our privilege and our adventure to discover our own special light.

— MARY DUNBAR

Pursue fun, new activities that interest you, like yoga, rock climbing, hiking, or gardening. Discovering new interests and passions will help you connect with yourself more deeply. Forget about the past and the future and just be present in the moment.

L augh

There's freedom in knowing you can carry joy and grief together.

— NANCY BERNS

Humor can play a healing role in a time of grieving. Studies have found that people who were able to smile and laugh when remembering a loved one demonstrated less anxiety and depressive symptoms as time passed. So, laugh and recall good times with your loved one and know that humor is a natural and very human part of healing.

G rief is challenging and brings with it many painful emotions. But over time, it has the power to transform our lives for the better as we struggle through it to become stronger, more resilient, and more loving toward ourselves. Practice gratitude, kindness and self-compassion. Discover new joy and passions. Find joy in small moments.

You are imperfect, you are wired for struggle, but you are worthy of love and belonging.

— BRENÉ BROWN

5

EXPLORE SPIRITUALITY

We are not human beings having a spiritual experience. We are spiritual beings having a human experience.

— PIERRE TEILHARD DE CHARDIN

After I lost my husband through divorce, I spent many nights in the darkness of my bedroom, full of fear, devastation, and grief.

I have lost everything I have ever known.

Life will never again be as it was.

Why did this happen?

There is nothing I can do to bring him back.

I felt haunted by all that was, and all that never would be. My heart broke at the thought of all the things we never got to do together, the life we would never know together. I was overwhelmed by anguish and loss. I missed so many things about my husband—his wisdom, his kindness, his patience...his shoulder to sleep on. I was deeply afraid of facing a life without him. I had never expected that life would turn out this way. It was never the plan.

Yet lying in the dark, in the most devastating moment of my life, when everything I knew had fallen away, something unexpected happened—something I will never quite be able to adequately capture in words.

I found God.

In the midst of grief, I felt God with me, walking with me, weeping as I wept. I surrendered and opened my heart to him, and when I did, I felt an overwhelming sense of love, comfort, and tenderness beyond words.

Prior to my life being touched with loss, I did not consider myself a spiritual person. Yet with loss, it was as if a switch had been turned on allowing me to awaken to my life in a profound way. By exploring my spirituality more deeply, I found I was able to feel hope in the midst of darkness, and joy and gratitude in even the most ordinary of moments. I no longer felt so alone. My spirituality transformed me as I began to heal and incorporate a deeper understanding and connection to suffering and loss into my life.

Spirituality is understanding that we are so much more than our minds or our bodies: our spirits are an integral part of who we are. The essence of spirituality is one of complete, unconditional love. Different than religion, it is an awareness that we are each connected to the energy of all creation—what I call God here, though others may have different names and faiths.

Loss often causes us to confront the questions that get at the very heart and meaning of life. As such, some may begin to experience a crisis of faith—questioning the very foundation of their lifelong beliefs or practices. Others may begin to explore this area of their lives for the first time.

These different spiritual responses to loss are natural. Whatever the response, it can be helpful to lean in to the confusion in order to understand your spiritual needs and path. Spirituality can be a great source of comfort, healing, and love when facing loss. You begin to find a deeper connection to your past and future and to see light in the darkness. Exploring your spiritual depths changes the core of who you are. You learn to move with the flow of your life and feel a renewed sense of hope and excitement about each coming moment.

HOW TO EXPLORE YOUR SPIRITUALITY

Spirituality is different for each person. For some it could involve connecting with a higher power, while for others, it could mean spending more time with your inner self to find peace and simplicity. This could mean practicing gratitude, spending time in nature, journaling, meditating, or praying—there are many ways to explore your spirituality. However you do it, know that cultivating this connection to yourself is worth the time. The following are a set of practices you can incorporate if you want to explore your spirituality:

ractice Gratitude

> *Gratefulness is the experience of the great fullness of life.*

— DAVID STEINDL-RAST

It can seem counterintuitive to be grateful in the darkest moments of your life. It can feel as if everything is lost, as if everything has been taken from you. Oddly, gratitude can help alleviate some of that pain and suffering. It can bring light into your world, as you see that there is still goodness and that life is full of simple blessings. You may start to see how much you took for granted and decide to live with gratitude for all life's simple joys and moments.

Gratitude will not change the pain of loss, but it can shift it into healing. It can transform your life from one filled with anger and bitterness to one filled with love and hope.

A simple way to start practicing gratitude is to spend 2-3 minutes each day writing in a gratitude journal, in which you give thanks to whoever or whatever you're grateful for. These could be simple things, like the taste of strawberries, vanilla ice cream, a warm day, good sleep, or a comforting friend. Try writing down at least one thing you are grateful for each day.

*L*et Go and Forgive

Forgiveness does not change the past, but it does enlarge the future.

— PAUL BOESE

We've all been hurt, and as we know, it can be hard to let go and forgive. When we have a hard time letting go of pain, it can cause problems in our lives, health, and relationships. Forgiveness doesn't mean forgetting what happened or making excuses. It just means letting go of suffering and moving on to a better place. It isn't easy, but it can come with time and daily practice. To forgive, try the following:

- Notice your emotions and let yourself feel them.

- Commit to letting go.

- Recognize what you can and cannot change or control.

- Focus on the present rather than the past.

- Release your emotions and allow peace to enter your life.

*W*ake to a Meditative Morning

The best and most beautiful things in the world cannot be seen nor even touched, but just felt in the heart.

— HELEN KELLER

When you feel ready, as soon as possible after you wake, spend time connecting to your breath. Simply be. It will calm you and help to release tension. This early morning time can help ground you, rooting your day in inner wisdom and intentionality.

*F*ind Solitude

Quiet the mind and the Soul will speak.

— MA JAYA SATI BHAGAVATI

An important aspect of healing is to spend some time in quiet solitude, away from the noise, demands, and busyness of life. With stillness, we connect with the higher power, that of goodness, kindness, peace, love, and wisdom, ultimately connecting with ourselves more deeply.

Many things flourish in solitude—reflection, peace, creativity, gratitude for the little things, our own voice and authenticity—all things that strengthen our spirit.

You can find solitude in many places, even in places that may be busy, such as an art gallery. Try disconnecting from electronics, phones, and computers. Get away, out of the house, and spend time in different places. Go into nature, attend local events, visit a coffee shop, practice yoga and meditation, or go for a drive. See what works best for you.

Connect with a Spiritual Teacher

There is no refuge from change in the cosmos, or from the heartbreak those changes can bring. But in the midst of all that is, was, or ever will be, there is a light that keeps shining, reaching us from far away.

— SASHA SAGAN

Speaking to a spiritual leader or teacher can help you understand loss and suffering in a broader sense. These mentors can help you along your spiritual journey toward continued growth and provide insight into how to explore and incorporate spirituality into your everyday life.

Pray

The darker the night, the brighter the stars,

The deeper the grief, the closer is God!

— FYODOR DOSTOYEVSKY, CRIME AND
PUNISHMENT

Praying can help you grow a spiritual connection to God—a power outside and bigger than yourself that you believe in. The great thing about prayer is that you can pray anytime and anywhere.

There are many different ways to pray. Prayer can involve conversations, but it can also be a time of contemplation and silent reflection. It can involve singing, praising, listening to music, or meditating. You can ask questions, make a request, speak, send good wishes, give thanks, or ask for things like strength. Sometimes, the most healing prayer is just to sit in silence.

ead Books That Will Shape Your Life

In a dark time, the eye begins to see.

— THEODORE ROETHKE

Spend time reading spiritual books—any books that help you explore your sense of a higher power and understanding of life and faith, or provide greater comfort, solace, and inspiration during difficult times. For a list of potentially helpful books, you can explore the spirituality section of your local bookstore or go online.

Here are a few books about spirituality to help you learn, grow, and find peace:

- *The Power of Now* by Eckhart Tolle. A book about how to live in the now, and how thoughts and emotions can get in the way of genuine peace and happiness. Tolle boils complicated concepts down to simple terms. This book radically changed my perspective on life, helped me let go of the past and taught me to live in the present moment.

- *A New Earth: Awakening to Your Life's Purpose* by Eckhart Tolle. An illuminating, uplifting book that describes how to live life in the present moment, and how to find life's meaning and purpose through transcending material possessions, unhappy relationships, and ego-based consciousness.

- *When Breath Becomes Air* by Paul Kalanithi. After a neurosurgeon is diagnosed with stage IV lung cancer and must confront his own mortality, he questions what makes life worth living. A profound and moving memoir.

- *The Untethered Soul: The Journey Beyond Yourself* by Michael A. Singer. Discusses how to let go of painful thoughts and emotions, how to cultivate a healthy, positive, and loving inner dialogue, and the peace and enlightenment that can come as a result.

- *The Language of God: A Scientist Presents Evidence for Belief* by Francis Collins. Written by the premier scientist who led the effort to decode the human genome, this memoir explores how science relates to faith and confronts some of the deepest questions of our time.

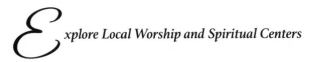

xplore Local Worship and Spiritual Centers

Truly, it is in the darkness that one finds the light, so when we are in sorrow, then this light is nearest of all to us.

— MEISTER ECKHART

Places like churches, temples, synagogues, mosques, and meditation retreats can help you nurture your spirituality and provide you with a sense of support and community. You can often find spiritual teachers at these places as well. Places of worship sometimes offer classes you can take to learn more about the beauty of different faiths. Many places of worship may also host support groups, where you can connect with others going through a significant loss.

 **ractice Creativity**

Art is a wound turned into light.

— GEORGES BRAQUE

Creativity has the power to soothe and restore us. It helps us spend time connecting to our spirit, and can help us release, process, and express emotions we may not even be aware we are experiencing. Through our creative work, we can find our voice and inner wisdom, and use them as sources of strength.

Explore different activities you enjoy, such as writing, singing, drawing, photography, poetry, or music. Find something that sustains and uplifts you, providing comfort and hope.

G et Away to the Outdoors

I believe that God is in me as the sun is in color and fragrance of a flower—the Light in my darkness, the Voice in my silence.

— HELEN KELLER

Being in nature can provide us with personal, authentic moments. In nature we can feel the restorative peace and presence of God or a higher power, as if we are walking in a cathedral of his creation. We feel greater clarity, connection, and peace as we become aware of the presence of nature and the universe, and our connection with all things.

Try gardening, visiting national or local parks or greenhouses, or taking a simple walk outside. Relax, observe your surroundings and enjoy the beauty—how delicate leaves look shifting in the wind, how light shines across the water. It will help open you up to a childlike sense of wonder.

Even though I walk through the darkest valley, I will fear no evil, for you are with me; your rod and your staff, they comfort me.

— PSALM 23:4 NIV

6

LOVE IN A NEW WAY

Grief, I've learned, is really just love. It's all the love you want to give,
but cannot. All that unspent love gathers up in the corners of your
eyes, the lump in your throat, and in that hollow part of your chest.
Grief is just love with no place to go.

— JAMIE ANDERSON

*W*e may be afraid that healing means letting go and losing our loved one forever, that it means we lose the memories we made, and the love we once shared.

But the truth is our loved ones will always be a deep part of us. Day by day, breath by breath, our task is to redefine our relationship with life and the people we've lost. We must learn to live and love in a new way now that our loved ones are no longer with us. Understanding the new form our love has taken can bring great

patients lost her husband of fifty years due to a heart

attack. Though the pain of his death was unbearable, she said one of the things that helped her continue to move forward was knowing he was still in her life, just in a different way. She knew he would always be a part of her.

In my own experience with grief over my divorce, although people told me to cut off all connection, I had a difficult time with that. We had created a healthy emotional distance after the divorce, but cutting off any sense of connection as if the past never existed caused my grief to get worse, not better.

A focus on moving on and letting go can make us feel as if we do not have the right to grieve. We may feel pressure, judgment, or shame for our natural, healthy responses to loss as our grieving may be seen as "holding on" or "dwelling on the past," and deemed unhealthy or sick.

Yet for the wounded, the grief and loss are very real. When losing someone you love, there is the pain of an altered future and what it means for your connection. With death, every day lived without them may feel like one in which your connection with them is gone. With divorces and breakups, seeing your ex live a future without you—getting remarried, starting a new family—may feel like your past connection has been invalidated or overwritten. This can be devastating, even if the divorce or breakup was desired.

It is natural for feelings of emotional connection to continue after losing someone you love. Many people can recall having feelings for partners long after the relationship is gone. Psychiatrist and family therapist Carl Whitaker proposed that just as it is not possible to end emotional connection to the family you grew up in, it is not possible to end an emotional connection to the family you created. Paradoxically then, loss can make you feel as if you are now required to break off an emotional connection that can't simply be turned off.

Indeed, increasing research suggests that it is natural for many people to miss loved ones and to feel a sense of continued connection with them. This work suggests that traditional models of grief, emphasizing a linear process of detachment and the severing of bonds to achieve a final state of "closure," are limited and primarily influenced by cultural values rather than actual grieving patterns. Instead, studies on grief conducted across cultures show that, for some people, finding ways to adjust and redefine that sense of a continued bond can be a healthy and adaptive part of the grieving process.

Like a Chinese finger trap, sometimes the more we struggle, the more stuck we become. Instead, we need to push our fingers in, accept things as they are, and honor the pain of grief and continued connection.

In my own case, all I could do was acknowledge that the loss would always be there. All I could do was honor all the things I had learned in the time we had together and carry that past wisdom and joy with me into the present and future, learning to love myself and others in new ways.

Healing and moving forward does not necessarily have to involve forgetting, compartmentalizing, or erasing the person you lost from your life. Instead, it means accepting the loss of that person, while also knowing that you can carry them with you, using the loss to grow more deeply in love, joy, and peace. It means accepting your ongoing, unfolding relationship with grief, so you can redefine your connection to the person and rewrite your story of loss. It means celebrating the love you experienced and feeling the pain and beauty of it while you welcome a new future.

HOW TO REDEFINE YOUR CONNECTION

When we are told to move on or to let go, we can become discon-nected from the wisdom, meaning, and connection that allowing grief can bring. But for many of us, there is no "finishing" when it comes to grief, just ongoing living and growing as we redefine our relationship to our lost loved ones, searching for meaningful ways to reconcile that connection with the life we continue to lead.

Everyone has different needs while grieving, depending on the personal nature of their grief and life situation. It is important to consider the impact a continued connection could have on you. If you think this strategy may not be helpful for you at this time, know that it's okay and return to it when you are ready. But if you think it would bring you greater peace to honor the past while embracing the future, try out the following strategies:

Find Meaningful Ways to Redefine Bonds

What we have once enjoyed deeply we can never lose. All that we love deeply becomes a part of us.

— HELEN KELLER

The reality of loss is that it may be impossible to forget and move on. To transform your grief, try redefining your connection to the person you lost. Redefine their role and place in your life so you can heal.

Releasing the past does not mean it never happened. It did. The person was in your life and will forever be a part of you. Letting go of the past just means learning to live in a new way, redefining your inner connection to that person within this new reality.

Find healthy and meaningful ways to redefine bonds with your loved one. This will help you release the past while being present and moving toward your future.

Here are some ways to honor your lost love:

- Create a memory box.

- Name a star after them.

- Donate money in their name to a worthy cause.

- Keep something they loved, such as a favorite pair of earrings, watch, or book.

- Choose your favorite photograph that reminds you of them and frame it.

- Create a photo book.

- Plant a tree, flower, or garden in a meaningful location.

- Dedicate a bench in their favorite spot.

- Purchase and release a butterfly in memory of them.

- Meditate and think of what advice they would give you.

- Choose an annual day to celebrate and remember them.

*S*pend Time in Reflection

The risk of love is loss, and the price of loss is grief. But the pain of grief is only a shadow when compared with the pain of never risking love.

— HILARY STANTON ZUNIN

Reflecting on how your loved one influenced your life can help you incorporate the past into your new reality. It can help you realize the way your loved one critically shaped your life and understand they will always be a part of you. Through reflection, you gain perspective and peace. Consider the following:

- How did they shape you?

- What are the different things they helped you learn?

- What was their importance to your life?

- How are you a different person today because of them?

- What are the good things in your future that will be different because of them?

*F*ace Unresolved Issues

They say time heals all wounds, but that presumes the source of the grief is finite.

— CASSANDRA CLARE

Losing someone we love can feel overwhelming, particularly when the person is taken away from us without warning. Such a loss doesn't make sense. We never had the chance to say good-bye.

If this is the case, think of different ways to say the things you wanted to say. Doing this can be very healing. Resolving the unresolved helps us incorporate the past into our new lives and identity. If you have something you need to say, find a way to release it.

For example, you could:

- Write a goodbye letter to release your emotions.

- Talk with them: Have a conversation with your loved one, imagining that they are sitting in the chair across from you. It may sound funny, but many have found this exercise to be very healing.

$\mathcal{B}$y redefining you connection to the person you lost, you can fully let go of what was and start thinking about what will be. Grief is simply love with nowhere to go. Allow the grief and the love to expand your heart. Give yourself permission to love—to honor the past while embracing the future.

Every love is carved from loss. Mine was. Yours is. Your great-great-great-grandchildren's will be. But we learn to live in that love.

— JONATHAN SAFRAN FOER

7

LEARN AND GROW

You will lose someone you can't live without, and your heart will be badly broken, and the bad news is that you never completely get over the loss of your beloved. But this is also the good news. They live forever in your broken heart that doesn't seal back up. And you come through. It's like having a broken leg that never heals perfectly—that still hurts when the weather gets cold, but you learn to dance with the limp.

— ANNE LAMOTT

*L*osing someone we love challenges the very foundation of our lives. It forces us to look at the deepest truths of our existence. We can find ourselves overcome with feelings of sadness, anger, shame, fear, and isolation.

Although our sense of connection to purpose and meaning in life may be lost, we have a choice about how to approach our grief. How we respond to it can make all the difference in whether we remain empty and embittered or live lives of greater understanding and wisdom.

Wisdom is not given to us. It can only be discovered. To find wisdom, we can actively turn toward our grief with compassion and a willingness to grow from the experience rather than become its victim. By asking ourselves what we are learning from our pain and suffering, we help ourselves put the pieces of our lives back together with intention, while also reflecting on the deepest sense of who we are, where we've been, and where we want to go.

Painful experiences never really go away, but we can learn to live with them and use them to open new doors, thus gaining a deeper understanding about love. Author Henri Nouwen wrote:

> Real, deep love is, as you know, very unobtrusive, seemingly easy and obvious, and so obvious that we take it for granted. Therefore, it is often only in retrospect—or better, in memory— that we fully realize its power and depth. Yes, indeed, love often makes itself visible in pain.

Nothing is the same after losing someone or something that you love greatly. And yet, in many ways, perhaps we are never more aware of what that love meant—and the preciousness of life itself —until it's gone.

Loss can reveal what is true and important to us and be a catalyst for personal transformation and inner growth, if we allow it. Through loss, we can become wiser and more alive.

HOW TO LEARN AND GROW FROM GRIEF

ᵽresents us with one of the most fundamental questions in w to deal with suffering. These feelings are very real and difficult. How do you take your suffering and transform it? How do you take grief and use it for good?

It's hard, painful work, struggling through grief. But know that you are not alone. Many of us have felt this kind of pain, hopelessness, and heartbreak, and have somehow made it through, growing stronger and wiser in the process. Here are a few ways to get started:

 *eflect on Life*

Wisdom comes only through suffering.

— AESCHYLUS, AGAMEMNON

Grief offers us an opportunity to pause and ask the deeper questions of life, so use this opportunity to reflect. Discover wisdom and pieces of yourself you never realized or had forgotten. By moving through loss and grief, you will begin to understand the inevitability of suffering and the preciousness of life itself.

Reflect on the following questions:

- What lesson are you taking with you from this loss? What will be its legacy?

- How has your understanding of life broadened after this loss?

- What is truly important in life?

- Did you make any mistakes? If so, how can you grow from them?

- What are some things you would like to do differently moving forward?

- Are there any ways this loss has helped or pushed you to grow for the better?

- What have you learned about yourself as a result of this loss that you wouldn't otherwise know?

- What do you want to result from your experience with loss?

- How can your experience with loss be used for good?

Take some time to reflect on these questions. Be honest with yourself as you answer them. Some of the answers may come to you over time.

 *ractice Acceptance*

> *Understanding is the first step to acceptance, and only with acceptance can there be recovery.*

> — J. K. ROWLING, HARRY POTTER AND THE
> GOBLET OF FIRE

It's hard to accept what you do not want to be true. You may think, "Things shouldn't be this way," or "This isn't fair." But resisting reality will not change the situation. It only leads to more pain and suffering, prolonging suffering and delaying healing.

Acceptance does not mean liking, agreeing with, or endorsing the current situation. It just means that you accept each moment as it is.

By practicing acceptance—that the loss is real, that things can no longer be as they were—you'll begin to move forward and heal.

Acceptance is a skill that can be learned and practiced. Take these steps:

- START SMALL: Try accepting small things each day. For example, accept that it is raining or that there is traffic today. Slowly but surely, you'll be able to accept more as time passes.

- GET A BROAD PERSPECTIVE: Try to see the present situation as the result of a million other decisions and events. Life involves a chain reaction of events going back in time, beginning far in the past before any of us were even born. Trying to fight the past only creates more suffering and blinds us to the present. The present is the only moment we have control over.

- MEDITATE: Meditating can help with accepting the present moment as it is, without judgment (see Chapter 1 for meditation exercises).

Take on New Challenges

The world breaks everyone and afterwards many are strong at the broken places.

— ERNEST HEMINGWAY, A FAREWELL TO
ARMS

After the loss of a loved one, you may have to take on responsibilities they formerly handled, such as finances, taxes, laundry, or cooking. Use this as an opportunity to learn new skills and knowledge.

Don't be afraid of making mistakes. If you need motivation, try having an accountability partner—someone who will join you in taking on the challenge. Carve out time in your schedule to make it happen, and enjoy the process of immersing yourself in a new experience.

ommit to Growth

> *When we are no longer able to change a situation, we are challenged to change ourselves.*

— VIKTOR E. FRANKL, MAN'S SEARCH FOR
MEANING

Grief is one of the hardest things you will ever have to go through. It can be tempting to get stuck in despair, apathy, or hopelessness. It helps to commit to a good outcome, to resolve to use this experience to become stronger and wiser.

To commit to growth, write down one to three goals you have for yourself. Try to make them as specific and as actionable as possible. For example, if you are interested in becoming more resilient, specific goals could be to practice mindfulness once a day, to practice positive affirmations each morning, or to spend time with friends once or twice per week, even if you don't feel like it.

Once you have goals in place, tell others about them to hold yourself accountable and take action!

Trust in the Journey

If you're going through hell, keep going.

— WINSTON CHURCHILL

Know that pain and sorrow will fade with time. How you are feeling now will not be how you feel next week, month, or year— that's just the nature of emotions. Trust that, with continued practice and effort, you can rebuild your life. Although the grief may feel unbearable and may become worse before it gets better, remember that your journey is ultimately leading you toward healing.

Loss changes us forever, developing and refining us like silver. Through grief, we learn the value of each moment and realize just how precious it is. We learn about faith and spirituality. We learn how to be present and how to savor time with our loved ones. We learn that suffering and loss are inevitable. We learn that both pain and joy can be experienced at the same time. We learn to love more deeply. We grow and become wiser.

In place of what is lost, something new emerges. It may not be what we imagined. But it is beautiful and it is ours.

— DANI SHAPIRO

8

FIND MEANING AND PURPOSE

In some way, suffering ceases to be suffering at the moment it finds a meaning, such as the meaning of a sacrifice.

— VIKTOR E. FRANKL, MAN'S SEARCH FOR
MEANING

*L*osing my husband brought me to a crossroads in my life. I realized I had a choice: to use the loss as a means to grow in consciousness, love, and faith, or to let the grief swallow me whole.

It wasn't an easy choice.

And it wasn't a decision that came instantly.

But ultimately, the loss of my husband created within me an intense desire and passion to live with greater intention, depth, meaning, and service to others.

Through grief, I realized that I wasted so much time in my life focused on my career, material possessions, anxieties, and other worldly concerns. If only I had known that certain moments would be the last. What I would do to go back in time and be present in those moments, to savor and delight in even our most ordinary days together.

Through grief, I saw that there was meaning to our lives all along: it was in those small moments and simple expressions of love.

When we lose someone we love, our fundamental sense of meaning is shattered. The loss undermines everything we thought we knew of our world, leading us to believe that life is meaningless. The most difficult losses are the ones that seem the most senseless.

Researchers Robert Neimeyer and Diana Sands wrote:

> In the aftermath of life-altering loss, the bereaved are commonly precipitated into a search for meaning at levels that range from the practical (How did my loved one die?) through the relational (Who am I, now that I am no longer a spouse?) to the spiritual or existential (Why did God allow this to happen?). How—and whether—we engage these questions and resolve or simply stop asking them shapes how we accommodate the loss itself and who we become in light of it.

Finding meaning in loss is thus a principal task in learning to live again. Questioning and making sense of the loss—focusing on the lessons learned and what the experience means about life in general—can help to turn otherwise meaningless suffering into an experience filled with meaning and purpose.

This task won't be easy. It will take patience and perseverance. But as we take it on, we find ourselves beginning to heal. We grow stronger and approach life with greater intention.

We begin to understand that there is a greater purpose to our pain. We see that we can use our experiences with suffering to contribute to the world and provide hope to others. For who better to help someone who has lost a loved one than someone who has experienced this pain themselves?

The things we may find most painful, terrible, and tragic can be the very things we can use for good in our lives and in the lives of others. Losing a loved one can cause us to think deeply about our priorities. It is an opportunity to spend the limited time we have left pursuing what's truly meaningful.

HOW TO FIND YOUR LIFE'S MEANING AND PURPOSE

When we lose the person we love, a void opens up in their place, forcing us to confront meaninglessness itself. Facing the absolute finality of the loss, it can be easy to get lost in our feelings and lose perspective on our greater purpose in life.

So how do we transcend despair and fill the void? The following are some actions that can help:

*K**eep a Journal*

Give sorrow words. The grief that does not speak

Whispers the o'erfraught heart, and bids it break.

— WILLIAM SHAKESPEARE, MACBETH

Writing can help you process your thoughts and emotions surrounding the loss of your loved one. Throughout history, people have turned to self-expression to get through grief and to gain a greater perspective. For instance, after losing his wife to cancer, writer C. S. Lewis wrote in journals to work through his grief and to articulate how it impacted his views on life, death, and faith.

There are different formats of journals: paper notebooks, apps, a simple document on the computer. Blogging is also a great way to journal, and you can control what level of privacy and information you are willing to share with others. To make journaling as easy as possible, you can write just a few bullets about each day.

 *ind Your Why*

He who has a why to live for can bear almost any how.

— FRIEDRICH NIETZSCHE

We are forever changed by loss. There is no turning back time or taking away the pain. Commit to making meaning from losing your loved one. For example, put more emphasis on your current relationships, reorder your life priorities, or resolve to use this experience to grow stronger. Sometimes people also take their experiences to begin a new life mission and inspire new contributions to the world. After her thirteen-year-old daughter was struck and killed by a drunk driver, Candy Lightener founded the organization Mothers Against Drunk Driving (MADD), which is now one of the most influential nonprofit organizations in the United States.

 *elp Others*

I have been burdened with glorious purpose.

— CAMILLE RANKINE

When you are ready, and when an opportunity presents itself, help others who are grieving loss. You understand grief and can identify with their pain and offer invaluable support. You don't need to solve everyone's problems—a friend probably doesn't want that and may just need someone to listen. By working to lessen their suffering, you will feel a greater purpose to your own suffering.

 *xpand Your Mind and Heart*

It is our job, our responsibility, perhaps even our sacred calling, to take whatever life has handed us.

— DANI SHAPIRO

Volunteering can be one way to expand your mind and heart. After losing his wife to breast cancer, a patient of mine began to volunteer for a local breast cancer association. He said volunteering served as a great balm for his grief, and doing this helped him see the needs of others. Through it, he stayed focused on other people and spent his time wishing for their happiness, just as he wished for his own. By stepping outside of our own lives, we see the bigger picture. We learn that there is nothing more fulfilling than using our own lives and stories as a source of good for others.

ove

May love be what you remember most.

— DARCIE SIMS

My friend's husband passed away from cancer many years ago. Though it was the darkest period of her life, she says grief ultimately caused her to shed those things that had no meaning. In the end, she only held onto the one valuable thing that really mattered: love. She came away from that experience realizing the importance of love and relationships, which deepened her love for others.

Love can take many different forms—you can love pets, friends, and family. And anything you do can be done with love—even simple things, like laundry, listening, writing a letter, cooking, and driving. It's all about intention. And you can always help someone in need, or tell your loved ones how much you love them.

Simplify your life and spend time with those you love. Continue developing your connection with others. Appreciate the fragility of life, and openly share your love for others.

arpe Diem

Take it from an old guy. The waves never stop coming, and somehow you don't really want them to. But you learn that you'll survive them. And other waves will come. And you'll survive them too. If you're lucky, you'll have lots of scars from lots of loves. And lots of shipwrecks.

— G. SNOW

Find wonder in small moments. Feel gratitude for the small blessings in your life. Find the meaning in your suffering, and use it to live a full life today. Take in all the light that surrounds you. See life for the gift that it is. Fall in love with life with all its pain, heartbreak, and awe-inspiring beauty.

*G*rief reveals a greater purpose and meaning to our lives. By embracing it, we grow and gain the wisdom we need to better our lives and the lives of others. We see that our suffering was not for nothing. We live more courageously and wholeheartedly. We live with more presence and gratitude for life itself. We smile and love more deeply. Hope becomes a part of us again. And it transforms us.

> *But when it's over and you're alone, you begin to see that it wasn't just a movie and a dinner together, not just watching sunsets together, not just scrubbing a floor or washing dishes together or worrying over a high electric bill. It was everything, it was the why of life, every event and precious moment of it.*

— DEAN KOONTZ, ODD HOURS

A LETTER FROM ME TO YOU

I am grateful to have taken this journey with you. There is a peace and hope to knowing we are not alone.

Healing after the loss of a loved one is not easy, but there is a beauty in the scar that results and a deepening in the love that remains.

Nothing is ever the same after the loss of a loved one. The life and world as we have known it are gone. A part of ourselves is lost, and we are forever changed—challenged to grow in a positive direction and to rediscover a life of love and meaning.

By using the methods described in this book and rising to meet this challenge, we can see that:

- darkness and sorrow can give rise to light and hope.

- to grieve is to love and to understand this is peace.

- through brokenness, our hearts can be transformed and healed.

- the meaning of life is love—to grow, delight, embrace, and be present for ourselves and for others.

- your time in this world is precious.

Grief is not something we ever really get past or over, but it is something we can transcend. I know that with time, love, and support, and through using the strategies in this book, you can heal and make it through.

Thank you for reading, for connecting. If you enjoyed reading this book and found it helpful, I'd sincerely appreciate it if you wrote a review on Amazon (https://www.amazon.com/dp/B0775FZ2VD) to allow this book to potentially help another person seeking life and meaning.

Thank you.

Best wishes,

Eleora Han

FREE BOOK RESOURCES

As a thank you to my readers, I have created a companion book download site with supplemental book resources, including:

- A list of 77 essential resources and hyperlinks to help you cope with grief and get support.

- A grief journal with 33 exercises, writing prompts, and reflections to help you find greater hope and healing.

To download these free book resources, please visit www.eleorahan.com/griefbookdownloads.

ABOUT THE AUTHOR

I am a clinical psychologist and writer. I am passionate about bringing healing to people struggling with difficult life events and stressors. I have spent the past eight years studying depression, stress, mood disorders, and vulnerability, writing and publishing extensively in leading peer-reviewed psychology and psychiatry academic journals, and collaborating with top researchers across the country. I have helped my patients, who include children, adults, and families, learn strength-and resilience-based skills to live lives of greater peace, wholeness, and joy.

As each person has different needs, I integrate best practices from a breadth of evidence-based treatments into my work, including cognitive behavioral therapy (CBT), dialectical behavior therapy (DBT), and mindfulness and acceptance-based approaches to best enhance the lives and well-being of my clients and readers.

My educational background includes a PhD in clinical psychology from the University of Maryland, followed by a clinical residency at Kennedy Krieger Institute and Johns Hopkins Hospital.

As a young student, when asked what I wanted to do with my career, my answer was clear: first, I want to write books that give rise to greater wisdom and hope, and second, I want to help bring research on emotional and behavioral health into actual, real-world practice to build a more promising future for individuals and families.

Thank you for helping me live this dream.

You can find me online here:

www.eleorahan.com

www.facebook.com/eleorahanauthor

www.twitter.com/eleorahan

www.pinterest.com/eleorahan

ACKNOWLEDGMENTS

This work would not have been possible without the support of many people. I would like to thank all of my patients and clients over the years, who have taught me so much about strength, resilience, grief, and loss. It has been a privilege to journey with you.

I would like to thank my parents for their love and support, and Arjun, my partner and best friend, who encouraged me with patience, joy, and love every step of the way, providing much inspiration.

A special thank you to my wonderful editor, Candace Johnson, for her belief in this project, her constant guidance, and brilliant feedback. To Jennifer Lane, Tish Peden, and Melissa Hauptman, thank you for reading early drafts and for your words of encouragement in the process.

Thank you also, to Sam, Ainslie, Jess, Judy, Isabelle, and Alvin, who were among the first to recognize and believe in me and cheered me on throughout my writing endeavors. To my mentor,

Lea, without whom I wouldn't be the writer, psychologist, scientist, researcher, or person I am today. To Marcee and my church family who served as lights to me in my time of darkness. To Jared, whose influence continues to live on in me, as evidenced throughout these pages.

NOTES

Bonanno, G. A. (2009). *The Other Side of Sadness: What the New Science of Bereavement Tells Us About Life After Loss.* New York, NY: Basic Books.

Bonanno, G. A., Galea, S., Bucciarelli, A., & Vlahov, D. (2007). "What predicts psychological resilience after disaster? The role of demographics, resources, and life stress." *Journal of Consulting and Clinical Psychology*, 75, 671– 682.

Gold, L. (2009). *Healthy Divorce: Keys to Ending Your Marriage While Preserving Your Emotional Well-Being.* Naperville, IL: Sourcebooks, Inc.

Gurman, A. S., Lebow, J. L., & Snyder, D. K. (Eds.). (2015). *Clinical Handbook of Couple Therapy* (5th ed). New York, NY: Guilford Press.

Emery, R. E., & Dinescu, D. (2015). *Separating, Divorced, and Remarried Families.* Handbook of Family Therapy (pp. 484–499). New York, NY: Routledge.

Epstein, R., Kalus, C., & Berger, M. (2006). "The continuing bond

of the bereaved towards the deceased and adjustment to loss."
Mortality, 11, 253-269.

Klass, D., Silverman, P. R., & Nickman, S. (Eds.). (2014). *Continuing Bonds: New Understandings of Grief*. New York, NY: Taylor & Francis.

Kübler-Ross, E. (1975). *Death: The final Stage of Growth*. Englewood Cliffs, NJ: Prentiss-Hall.

Kübler-Ross, E., & Kessler, D. (2014). *On Grief and Grieving: Finding the Meaning of Grief Through the Five Stages of Loss*. New York, NY: Scribner.

Neff, K. (2003). "Self-compassion: An alternative conceptualization of a healthy attitude toward oneself." *Self and Identity*, 2, 85–101.

Neimeyer, R. A. (2006). "Bereavement and the quest for meaning: Rewriting stories of loss and grief." *Hellenic Journal of Psychology*, 3, 181–188.

Neimeyer, R.A. & Sands, D.C. (2011). "Meaning reconstruction in bereavement: From principles to practice. In Neimeyer, R.A., Harris, D.L., Winokuer, H.R. & Thornton, G.F. (Eds.) *Grief and bereavement in contemporary society: Bridging research and practice* (pp. 9–22). New York, NY: Routledge.

Shear, M. K., Simon, N., Wall, M., Zisook, S., Neimeyer, R., Duan, N., ... & Gorscak, B. (2011). "Complicated grief and related bereavement issues for DSM–5." *Depression and Anxiety*, 28, 103–117.

Made in the USA
Middletown, DE
16 November 2020

24222236R00061